THE PITKIN GUI
THE HOLOC

C000148859

Chris McNab

Antisemitism has a long, dark history. Expelled from their ancestral lands in Israel after they rose up against the Roman occupiers in CE 69–70, Jews settled where they could, spreading from the Middle East and Mediterranean, and settling in mainland Europe in the 10th century. Yet the medieval European Church used perceived Jewish involvement in Christ's crucifixion as a false peg upon which to hang centuries of anti-Jewish suspicion and hatred.

European Jewry occupied a complex social position from the early Middle Ages. It came to be valued for its commercial activity, particularly its expertise in finance and international commerce. Yet older, more sinister moods persisted, bolstered by jealousy of perceived Jewish wealth and Jewish resistance to Christian assimilation. Periodic, localized violence towards Jews was not uncommon, occasionally expanding to outright officially approved massacres. Alternative persecutions included confiscation of property and businesses, or forced segregation in separate zones of towns and cities. Such aggression kept the Jewish people on the move, large numbers being displaced into Eastern Europe,

particularly Poland and the Russian Empire. In turn, persecution there returned many Jews to Western Europe during the 1800s, Germany and Austria-Hungary being popular destinations in the later part of the 19th century.

Yet by the early 20th century, it appeared that antisemitism had been tempered. Enduring enlightenment values, secularization, increased intermarriage between religions and political tolerance had made life for European Jews stable. So why is it, therefore, that between 1941 and 1945 six million Jews were murdered in an act of systematic, industrial slaughter? Here we explain how Germany – one of Europe's most civilized countries – was the perpetrator of what is one of history's most profound crimes against humanity.

ABOVE: Barbed wire at the Auschwitz concentration camp – today a living museum to the Holocaust – hangs in front of the Star of David on the Israeli flag.

LEFT: Railway lines lead directly into the main entrance to Auschwitz II, Birkenau, extermination camp. More than one million people were murdered in Auschwitz between 1940 and 1945.

FRONT COVER: A poignant memorial in Auschwitz shows empty uniforms of the type worn by prisoners.

Antisemitism in Germany: 1900–1933

In the early 20th century, the status of Germany's 520,000 Jews appeared assured. Many held respectable positions in society as businessmen, civil servants and financiers. Intermarriage with non-Jews became more commonplace – one in four German Jews were marrying non-Jews by the 1920s. Life, on the whole, was good.

Against this backdrop of assimilation, however, were deep undercurrents of antisemitism. Its roots were religious, but by the early 20th century the hostility was strapped more to concepts of race, evolution and nationalism. German anti-Jewish philosophers saw Jews as enemies of national unity, particularly through their perceived associations with communism. Conversely, social problems such as poverty were frequently blamed on Jewish capitalism. More insidiously, antisemitic writers used wild concepts of biological destiny (often by contorting Darwin's theory of evolution) to argue that Jews were contaminating the so-called pure and superior German *Volk*. Garish literary caricatures presented the Jewish people as evil, alien creatures, sucking the lifeblood out of the citizenry.

In 1918 Germany was defeated in the First World War, having shed two million lives fighting a seemingly pointless conflict. The German surrender, and the subsequent harsh peace terms imposed on Germany by the Allies, left a bitter aftertaste in many mouths. German society became more harshly split along left- and right-wing political lines. The German right explained their country's defeat as the result of having been 'stabbed in the back' by a Jewish-dominated, communist-oriented faction that was plotting its own control of the state. The theory also argued that the Jewish people had been financially feathering their nests while German soldiers died on the battlefronts – forgetting the 100,000

BELOW: Jewish culture was vibrant in many places throughout Europe. Here we see Jews of Lodz, Poland's second largest city. Lodz had a pre-war Jewish population of 233,000, which constituted about a third of the city's entire population.

Jewish culture in Germany

The Nazi persecution of the Jewish people flew in the face of the impressive contribution Jews made to German culture. In the field of music, Germany's Jewish community produced legendary composers such as Arnold Schoenberg, Paul Hindemith and Kurt Weill. Jewish athletes were amongst the best the country had to offer, including boxer Erich Seelig, tennis player Daniel Prenn (Germany's top-ranked player), high jumper Gretel Bergmann and fencer Helene Mayer – nine Jewish athletes won medals in the 1936 Berlin Olympics. In the world of art, German Jewish artists such as Max Beckman, Max Ernst and Paul Klee had been at the forefront of the expressionist and surrealist movements. Many prominent Jewish figures emigrated in the 1930s under the growing pressures of persecution and discrimination.

ABOVE: A supplement to the German Jewish newspaper *Jüdische Rundschau* promotes Jewish emigration to Palestine. More than 60,000 Jews left Germany for Palestine during the 1930s.

Jews who served, and 13,000 who were killed, as frontline soldiers, many of whom were decorated for bravery.

Antisemitism therefore sharpened in Germany during the Weimar Republic (republican Germany between 1919 and 1933). Furthermore, during the 1920s it also found voice through a new, rising organization – the *Nationalsozialistische Deutsche Arbeiterpartei* (NSDAP; National Socialist German Workers' Party), or Nazi Party. Led by a young war veteran, Adolf Hitler, the NSDAP was virulently anti-Jewish, but also offered a political programme that from the late 1920s increasingly appealed to a German public hungry for economic, political and military reform. As a result, through a democratic electoral process the Nazis rose to power, and Hitler took the position of German Chancellor in 1933. From this point the antisemitism present within German society was destined to become a centrepiece of government policy.

RIGHT: The hateful Nazi propaganda weekly paper *Der Stürmer* was established in 1927 and at its peak in 1935 reached a circulation of about 480,000 copies per week. It was full of anti-Jewish articles and imagery – here Nazi swastikas are shown raining down on caricatures of Jews. The text at the bottom of the page translates: 'The Jews are our misfortune!'

Hitler's Racial War

Having served his country with distinction in the First World War, the 29-year-old Adolf Hitler was incensed, and politically radicalized, by Germany's surrender in 1918. He joined the NSDAP, and rose rapidly through its hierarchy by a mixture of talented oratory and passionate nationalism. In 1921 he became the Party's Führer (leader), but in 1924 was jailed for nine months following the Beer Hall putsch in Munich – the NSDAP's premature attempt to seize power. During his imprisonment, he wrote his personal political philosophy in *Mein Kampf* ('My Struggle') which, once he was released, on 20 December 1924, became an ideological guidebook for the rising NSDAP.

Aided by the turmoil of the Great Depression – which crippled much of the German economy in the late 1920s and early 1930s – the Nazis rode a wave of social discontent to become the largest political party in Germany by 1932. Through adept political manoeuvring, and the bullying presence of Hitler's *Sturmabteilung* (SA: Storm Detachment) and *Schutzstaffel* (SS: Protection Squadron) paramilitary guards, Hitler took the office of Chancellor in 1933. The following year,

ABOVE: A German boy sits on a park bench in Germany, c.1935. The words painted on the back of the seat translate as 'Only for Aryans', a clear sign of how Jews were being pushed out of even the simplest aspects of public life, such as sitting on a bench in the open air.

when President von Hindenburg died, Hitler took over as Führer of all Germany. Political opposition was progressively banned, and Hitler became an uncontested dictator.

LEFT: Hitler claimed *Mein Kampf*, the first volume of which was published in 1925, was autobiographical. He originally intended the title to be 'Four and a Half Years of Struggle against Lies, Stupidity, and Cowardice'.

The 'Aryan master race'

The notion of an 'Aryan master race' was at the core of Nazi racialist theory, although it has no basis in science or sociology. It developed in the 19th century, and was based around the fallacious belief that not only were white races superior to non-whites, but there was also a hierarchy within the whites themselves. At the very summit of this supposed hierarchy, displaying superior culture, values, martial traditions and physical attributes, were the 'Aryans'. The Aryans were defined vaguely as Nordic-European peoples, although the Nazis believed that the Germans were naturally the most superior race. In Nazi eyes, the perfect Aryan specimen was tall, strong, blonde, hardened and resolute; Jews were ridiculously caricatured as the very antithesis of this model – sickly, dark, deceptive, physically stunted. The model of Aryan physicality informed Nazi propaganda, education and later racial policies, although there were many anomalies – Adolf Hitler himself was a long way from being of Aryan appearance.

ABOVE: Nazi ideology was heavily focused on producing a warlike and hardened youth to fit with the Aryan identity. Here boys of the *Hitlerjugend* (Hitler Youth) practice throwing hand grenades at a camp in Quedlinburg.

Notions of race were central to Hitler's leadership and philosophy. In essence, he claimed that almost every race of people was driven by the primordial urge to reproduce and to expand territorially. This meant that war was natural for Germany, as it attempted to acquire the *Lebensraum* (living space) that was its manifest destiny. For Hitler, however, Jews were an exception to this world view. He claimed they did not possess their own territory, but instead lived in a 'parasitical' relationship with their (German) host. Hitler literally dehumanized the Jewish people in his writings, presenting them almost as hostile alien beings eating away at society from the inside. His view, without any rational basis, was that German people were also at risk from interbreeding with Jews, polluting what he saw as Aryan purity (see panel).

Historians diverge, often bitterly, over Hitler's long-term intentions towards Jewish people. Some argue that murdering the Jews was always Hitler's goal, while others say we can only see this in hindsight, and that the plan to exterminate Jews developed more haphazardly and by increments. This is a complex debate that remains unresolved. What is certain, however, is that once the Nazis were in power, the persecution of Jews was to begin in earnest.

ABOVE: A poster from 1938 depicts the Nazi ideal of an Aryan family. Hitler and his followers were obsessed with false notions of racial 'purity', which the Nazis believed was threatened by the Jews.

Persecution Begins: 1933–1939

Once in power, the Nazis began implementing antisemitic legislation. In April 1933, the first major enactment banned Jews from the practice of law, while the innocuously titled 'Law for the Restoration of the Civil Service' began ousting Jews from government office, a process complete by November.

Other laws came rapidly. Over the next six years Jews were banned from journalism, dentistry, medicine (human and veterinary), universities and academies, military service, professional arts and teaching. On 1 April 1933, Hitler also launched an attempted boycott of Jewish shops (the first of many), backed by intimidation from members of the *Sturmabteilung*. Revealingly, the boycott was far less successful than hoped, indicating that the German population at large was not as antisemitic as Hitler believed. Furthermore, from 1934 pressure on Jewish businesses relaxed somewhat – Jewish tax revenues were temporarily deemed too important for the German economy to crush entirely. Nevertheless, the combined effects of the persecution meant that by 1936 a full 45 per cent of Jews were either living on benefits or from their savings. From 1937, however, when Hitler's

ABOVE: A group of *Sturmabteilung* (SA) – a Nazi organization also known as the 'brownshirts' because of the colour of their uniforms – block the entrance to the Jewish-founded Woolworth department store in Berlin in April 1933. Those who attempted to go inside the building risked violence and intimidation.

LEFT: Hitler Youth members paste boycott signs on windows of Jewish businesses in Austria in 1938. Typical signs read 'Don't buy from the Jews!' and 'The Jews are our misfortune', and such campaigns were backed by lurid, invented stories in the press about supposed Jewish crimes.

ABOVE: Some of the early inmates of Dachau concentration camp, located near Munich in southern Germany, are forced to do manual labour. Dachau was established for 'political prisoners' in March 1933 and became a 'model' for many subsequent camps.

The Nuremberg Race Laws

The Nuremberg Race Laws were enacted around the time of the Nazi Party's Nuremberg rally in 1935. The two major pieces of legislation were the 'Law for the Protection of German Blood and German Honour' and the 'Reich Citizenship Law'. The former prohibited marriage between Jews and non-Jews, forbade Jews from displaying the German flag and stopped Jews employing German females under the age of 45 as domestic servants. The latter, more significantly, reclassified Jews as subjects rather than citizens of the German state. These laws were progressively tightened by subsequent decrees, which went on to classify degrees of Jewishness according to a complex series of racial and ancestral calculations. All these calculations were without foundation, such as classifying a person's 'race' according to nonsensical links to his or her grandparents' religion. What such laws did was place Jews at the mercy of a government that was not constitutionally bound to grant them any form of human rights.

right-hand man, Hermann Göring, took over the Finance Ministry, Jewish assets were remorselessly plundered. A law of April 1938 ordered all Jewish assets over 5,000 Reichsmark to be registered and put at the disposal of the German government.

The Nazis also enacted a series of so-called racial purity laws during the pre-war period. The most important were the Nuremberg Race Laws of September 1935 (see panel), which essentially stripped Jews of German citizenship and civil rights. However, the German people did not give universal support for such persecution. Christian organizations such as the 'Confessing Church' publicly stated their objections, and many conservative politicians expressed concern. Yet during the late 1930s, with Germany on the verge of war, opponents were purged from influential office and the hardline Nazis consolidated control. Those Germans who either supported or were associated with Jews could find themselves arrested and imprisoned. Moreover, the Nazis pushed ahead developing a network of concentration camps – the first were established at Dachau, Oranienburg, Lichtenburg and Esterwegen shortly after the Nazis came to power. Although the camps were originally intended for political prisoners, from about 1938 they quickly began to receive hundreds of Jews charged with recently invented racial and social 'crimes'. By 1939, 50,000 people were imprisoned, laying some of the groundwork for the far darker camps of the future.

ABOVE: A poster advertising 'The Eternal Jew' exhibition held in Munich from November 1937 to January 1938, which served to increase antisemitic views.

Life for German Jews: 1933–1939

Responses to the rising antisemitism amongst the German Jews themselves were varied and complicated. There was a prevalent expectation that matters would eventually improve, a belief that this outpouring of traditional anti-Jewish sentiment would recede, just as it had in times past. The Jewish composer Kurt Weill said: 'I consider what is going on here so sickening that I cannot imagine it lasting more than a couple of months ... But one could be very wrong.'

To the optimistic, there was some evidence to support this conclusion. Nazi Germany was actually governed by a combination of state and party institutions. While the latter were implacably opposed to the Jewish people, the former were frequently more moderate.

ABOVE: A youth carries away the Star of David following the destruction of a Munich synagogue during *Kristallnacht* ('Night of Broken Glass'), a series of attacks on Jewish people and property throughout Nazi Germany on the night of 9–10 November 1938.

State authorities sometimes intervened to stop, or limit, Nazi violence towards Jewish people or property. Persecution also relaxed slightly around the time of the Berlin Olympics in 1936 (Jewish athletes even competed), the Nazis wanting to present a golden image to the rest of the world.

Yet while the positives may have provided slight reassurance, conditions were becoming truly awful by the late 1930s. Jews were mocked or intimidated openly in the streets. Jewish children suffered untold bullying and racial abuse from other children and teachers alike; entire classes were devoted to teaching Nazi racial theory. From August 1938, all Jews had to carry the middle name Israel or Sarah as identifying terms, and from the following October Jewish passports were also marked with a 'J'.

Violence against Jews by SA or SS thugs became commonplace, and prosecutions – even for murder – were rare. On 9–10 November 1938, the Nazi state sanctioned a night of open violence against Jewish communities throughout Germany, in response to the shooting of a German embassy official, Ernst vom Rath, in Paris by a 17-year-old Polish Jew. In total, 91 Jews were murdered, 200 synagogues burned down and 7,500 Jewish businesses destroyed. As many as 30,000 Jewish men were deported to the concentration camps. Afterwards, the Nazis even imposed a 1,000 million Reichsmarks fine on the Jewish community for the murder of vom Rath.

For many Jews life in Germany had now become intolerable, and they chose emigration instead. During the 1930s, a total of 100,000 Jews went to the United States, 65,000 to Britain

ABOVE: A Jewish lawyer, Dr Michael Siegel, is publicly humiliated by Nazis on the streets of Munich in March 1933. The sign worn around his neck displays the words: 'I will never again file a complaint against the police', a clear indication that the Jews no longer enjoyed the protection of the state.

and more than 150,000 to Palestine. Others went to France, or as far afield as South America. As we shall explore later, Jewish emigration was an early stage in Hitler's attempt to force Jews from German life. Yet hundreds of thousands more remained by either choice or optimism that life would get better; but from 1939, with the onset of war, their lives became more horrific than anyone could have imagined.

ABOVE: The aftermath of *Kristallnacht*; German citizens walk past Jewish shops destroyed by Nazi thugs. The costs of repair for Jewish businesses and homes exceeded 4 million Reichsmarks.

RIGHT: In September 1939 the *Reichssicherheitshauptamt* (RSHA: Reich Main Security Office) even went so far as to ban the Jewish ownership of radios. Here officials inspect confiscated radio sets, which were taken without any form of financial compensation.

Everything changed for Europe's Jews with the German invasion of Poland in 1939, and the subsequent onset of the Second World War. From the beginning of the war until December 1941, Germany conquered Poland, Scandinavia, most of continental Western Europe, the Balkans and huge expanses of the western Soviet Union. Suddenly, millions more Jews fell under the control of the Third Reich.

What to do with these Jews posed a logistical and ideological problem for the Nazis. Two policies were therefore adopted: containment and extermination. In terms of containment, the Germans began to concentrate hundreds of thousands of Jews in ghettos in the General Government, the Nazi-controlled territory in

Heinrich Himmler

Heinrich Himmler arguably stands as the leading architect of the Holocaust. Born in 1900 near Munich, Himmler grew to control both the SS and the Third Reich's entire police and security services. A fanatical Nazi, but also a proficient bureaucrat, Himmler was devoted to fulfilling Hitler's wishes, and personally oversaw much anti-Jewish policy from 1933 to 1945. Through his deputy, Reinhard Heydrich, Himmler initiated the 'Final Solution' and on several occasions he personally witnessed Jewish executions taking place. Ironically, these nauseated him, but he had no qualms about organizing mass murder. Captured by the Allies following the German defeat, he committed suicide by taking a cyanide capsule on 23 May 1945.

RIGHT: Heinrich Himmler, one of the leading figures behind the design and execution of the 'Final Solution'. In the last months of the war, Himmler made some half-hearted efforts to 'trade' surviving Jews with the Allies, but nothing could mask the enormity of his horrific crimes.

ABOVE: A Jewish man kneels by a mass grave, about to be shot by a soldier of *Einsatzgruppe* D in Vinnitsa, Ukraine. Although under the authority of the SS, the *Einsatzgruppen* contained many different types of personnel, including police officers and civilian helpers and officials.

occupied Poland. Life in the disease-ridden ghettos was dreadful – possibly 500,000 Jews died there even before the 'Final Solution' was implemented (see pages 12–13). Yet the constant influx of Jews, including German Jews, into the ghettos meant that space simply ran out. Consequently, there were several instances of mass shootings of Jews – hundreds at a time – just to make room for other human 'consignments'.

Even more appalling, however, were the activities of the SS *Einsatzgruppen* (Task Commands). Formed in 1938 from various security service and SS personnel, these military-style units were in 1939 officially tasked with 'the annihilation of the Jews, Gypsies and political commissars'. Following behind the advance of the regular German Army (which was also far from innocent of crimes against Jews), the *Einsatzgruppen* conducted hundreds of outright extermination operations, rounding up Jewish communities and citizens and executing them or forcing them into ghettos. After the invasion of the Soviet Union in June 1941, these actions reached shocking levels. In 1941–42 alone, some 1.4 million Jews were forced at gunpoint

into ravines, fields or woodland and murdered. The killing operations could last for days, and did not discriminate between men, women or children. For example, on 29–30 September 1941, *Einsatzgruppe* C murdered 33,771 people in the ravine of Babi Yar near Kiev, Ukraine.

Yet shooting was, to the Nazi mind, a prolonged, violent business that drained military manpower, so alternative methods of mass execution were sought. The Nazis were also concerned about their men being traumatized from shooting hundreds of people, including children, at close range. From September 1941, therefore, gas vans were introduced on the Eastern Front. These were fitted with hermetically sealed cargo boxes into which Jews were forced and carbon monoxide gas pumped directly inside from the running engine. It usually took 15 agonizing minutes for the people inside to die, before their bodies were burned or dumped in ditches. Combined with the fact that by the autumn of 1941 the Nazis were no longer seeking Jewish emigration, the activities of the *Einsatzgruppen* indicated that Hitler and the Nazi hierarchy were about to reach what they called the 'Final Solution to the Jewish question'.

ABOVE: A gas van, used at Chelmno extermination camp for the murder of Jews. The invention of the gas van was largely the responsibility of SS Brigadeführer Artur Nebe, commander of *Einsatzgruppe* B. The largest such vans could kill up to 150 people at a time.

RIGHT: This map shows the Nazis' advance on the Soviet Union (Operation *Barbarossa*) that began on 22 June 1941, and the operational areas of the *Einsatzgruppen*.

Einsatzgruppe A: Baltic Republics
Einsatzgruppe B: Belorussia
Einsatzgruppe C: Northern and central Ukraine
Einsatzgruppe D: Bessarabia, southern Ukraine, Crimea, Caucasus

German advance
Extent of advance, December 1942
1 Army Group North
2 Army Group Centre
3 Army Group South

FINLAND
Leningrad
ESTONIA
LATVIA
Baltic Sea
LITHUANIA
Moscow
SOVIET UNION
BELORUSSIA
Smolensk
Kursk
GENERAL GOVERNMENT
GREATER GERMANY
Kiev
CZECHOSLOVAKIA
UKRAINE
Stalingrad
AUSTRIA
HUNGARY
BESSARABIA
ROMANIA
CRIMEA
CAUCASUS
Black Sea
BULGARIA
ALBANIA
TURKEY
GREECE

0   500 m
0   500 km

Designing the 'Final Solution'

The introduction of the gas vans on the Eastern Front in 1941–42 was not the first time this style of killing had been tested by the Nazis. From 1939 the Nazis began a programme of killing mentally and physically disabled adults and children (other groups who did not fit in with Nazi racial policy). This programme, known as *Aktion T4* (Action T4), initially had varied methods of murder. Sometimes victims were given lethal injections, or simply left to starve in their government-run institutions. Yet, steadily, carbon monoxide gassing, whether in vans or in fake shower blocks, became the norm. Between January 1940 and August 1941, a total of 70,273 people were murdered in this fashion.

Aktion T4 would become the experimental bedrock of the Holocaust. In July 1941, Reichsmarschall Hermann Göring sent a message to the chief of Germany's *Reichssicherheitshauptamt* (RSHA: Reich Main Security Office), which commissioned its chief, Reinhard Heydrich, 'to carry out all preparations with regard to organizational, factual and financial viewpoints for a total solution of the Jewish question in those territories in Europe under German influence.' 'Total solution', as history would show, was nothing more than a euphemism for the murder of an entire people.

Heydrich, a ruthless Nazi, arranged a meeting of key party and government officials at a lakeside

ABOVE: Reinhard Heydrich was head of the *Reichssicherheitshauptamt* and chairman of the Wannsee Conference in January 1942. He was wounded in Prague in an assassination attempt on 27 May 1942 and died from his injuries on 4 June.

RIGHT: The first page of the Wannsee Conference Protocol, which began by listing those in attendance. The document, dated 20 January 1942, gave a formal structure to the extermination of Jewish people in Germany and the occupied territories.

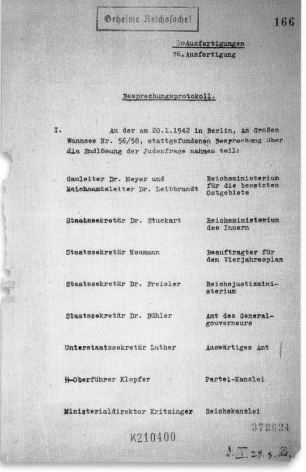

villa in the Berlin suburb of Wannsee. It was there, in a conference lasting only 90 minutes, that the Nazi Party put in place a coordinated programme for the concentration, deportation and murder of European Jewry. Minutes were taken by SS officer Adolf Eichmann, head of the Department for Jewish Affairs in the Gestapo and also one of the architects of the Holocaust. The minutes used terms such as 'emigration' and 'evacuation', which actually meant deportation and execution, as testified by Eichmann himself at his trial in 1961. The overall decision was to deport Jews from the occupied territories to 'the East' (Poland), where they would be placed in labour camps or simply executed (see panel). Labour camps themselves would be a source of attrition, the malnourished inmates worked to death in service of the Reich.

There is some ambiguous language in what we know as the Wannsee Protocol but, taken in context with all other evidence from the period, including from people who attended the conference and the fact that Chelmno extermination camp was already in operation, the meaning was clear. Although there is no record of a definitive written directive from Hitler ordering the 'Final Solution', such an order was unnecessary – Hitler's racial views were obvious, and it was largely left up to his administration to implement his oral commands. They did so with brutal efficiency.

The Wannsee Protocol

This central passage from the minutes of the Wannsee Conference highlights, in language stripped of all humanity, two possible destinies for Jews held by the Nazis:

> Under proper guidance, in the course of the 'Final Solution', the Jews are to be allocated for appropriate labour in the East. Able-bodied Jews, separated according to sex, will be taken in large work columns to these areas for work on roads, in the course of which a large portion will be eliminated by natural causes. The possible final remnant will, since it will undoubtedly consist of the most resistant portion, have to be treated accordingly, because it is the product of natural selection and would, if released, act as the seed of a new Jewish revival ... In the course of the practical implementation of the 'Final Solution', Europe will be combed through from west to east.

BELOW: The lakeside villa that was the venue for the Wannsee Conference. Today, the house acts as a memorial, museum and educational centre for Holocaust studies, in memory of those who paid dearly for the decisions taken here.

Death Camps

The Nazi concentration camp system contained several different kinds of institution. Extermination camps, for example, were little more than killing centres, designed specifically to murder thousands of Jews, Gypsies and other peoples with industrial efficiency. Labour camps, by contrast, basically used the prisoners as unpaid slave labour for the Reich, there to be worked and starved to death at the will of their gaolers. (Note that some camps, such as Majdanek and Auschwitz, combined both extermination and labour facilities.)

By the time the Wannsee Conference took place, extermination camps were already in development, with all the major examples concentrated in Nazi-occupied Poland. (There were some that the Nazis deemed 'minor' death camps in places such as Serbia, Croatia, Belorussia and Ukraine.) Gassing experiments had taken place in Auschwitz in September 1941, and in

ABOVE: A prisoner is photographed on arrival at a concentration camp. Along with other indignities suffered, all new prisoners would have a number tattooed on their forearm by which they would be recognized, part of the Nazi dehumanizing tactics in an effort to take away an individual's identity.

ABOVE: This map indicates the position of the main death camps, concentration camps and ghettos.

December 1941 mass gassings of Jews from the Lodz ghetto began at nearby Chelmno (Kulmhof). These were the first steps in Operation *Reinhard*, the murder of two million Jews from the General Government. By 1943, however, there were six major extermination camps: Auschwitz-Birkenau (Auschwitz II), Belzec, Chelmno, Majdanek, Sobibor and Treblinka, which received Jews from across occupied Europe.

The process by which people were murdered varied according to place and resources, but typically worked along the following lines. Consignments of Jews would arrive by train after a nightmarish journey of days without food or water, packed with suffocating tightness into cattle cars: these journeys alone claimed thousands of lives. If the people arrived at an extermination camp, they would immediately be sent to the gas chambers. If they arrived at a combined extermination/labour camp, by contrast, Nazi doctors would separate out those who could work (but who would be killed or die later), from those who would be murdered straight away. The latter typically included women with children, the children themselves, the elderly and the infirm. The Jewish arrivals were deprived of all their possessions, divided into the sexes, had their heads shaved (the purpose being that the hair was used in clothing manufacture), then told to strip naked, usually under the pretence of a 'delousing' shower. The victims were then forced, hundreds at a time, into 'shower rooms', where they were

Camp arrival

Barbara Stimler, an Auschwitz survivor, recounts her experience of arrival at the camp:

They didn't let us take the clothes at all, they started separating women from men. Cries. It was just terrible. The husbands were from wives, the mothers from sons, it was just a nightmare. I started to get diarrhoea, I was sick and diarrhoea, suddenly. We started going through the … through the gate; the SS men were on both sides. And the girls, young people that could see what state I was in, they had a bit of sugar and they started putting sugar in my mouth to revive me … And can you imagine the screams, the … the mother was going to the left, the daughter was going to the right, the babies going to the left, the mothers going to the right, or the mothers went together with the babies … Can you imagine?

gassed to death either by carbon monoxide from diesel motors or by Zyklon-B cyanide gas.

What is notable is that for the Nazis killing became a heavily administrated, industrialized process. Essentially, the camps were ghastly factories of death. At the peak of their 'efficiency', some camps were killing and cremating thousands of men, women and children a day, every day. By the end of 1942, almost all of Nazi-occupied Poland's Jews had been murdered.

ABOVE: Jews sent to the concentration camps were stripped of all their possessions, often including their clothing. Here a prisoner at a camp near Natzviller, France, sorts through huge piles of confiscated clothes and shoes. Some Nazi organizations became extremely wealthy through looted Jewish goods.

ABOVE: A gas chamber at Majdanek extermination camp near Lublin, Poland. The blue stains on the walls are deposits from Zyklon-B, which was the trade name for a lethal cyanide-based pesticide. Note the peep hole in the door, through which the guards could watch those inside dying.

Auschwitz

All concentration and extermination camps were terrible places, yet the name Auschwitz stands out as virtually synonymous with the Holocaust. Auschwitz was in many ways the ultimate expression of the 'Final Solution', a vast, sprawling camp system that between 1940 and 1945 murdered 1.1 million Jews, plus 150,000 Poles, 23,000 Gypsies, 15,000 Soviet prisoners of war (POWs) and around 25,000 other unfortunate inmates.

Located 250km (155 miles) south-west of Warsaw, Auschwitz was established in 1940. Originally it was purely a labour camp for Polish political prisoners, but in the late summer of 1941 its commander, Rudolf Höss, was tasked by Himmler to transform Auschwitz into the Third Reich's principal extermination camp for the murder of Jews from occupied Europe and the Soviet Union. Up until 1943 Auschwitz lagged behind most extermination camps in terms of aggregate numbers killed, but Höss oversaw the camp's expansion into a killing factory that eventually dwarfed all other camps.

By the end of 1943 Auschwitz was separated into three main compounds. Auschwitz I (the original camp) and Auschwitz III were both labour camps, the latter consisting of a major industrial centre at nearby Monowitz. The labour camps were populated by tens of thousands of Russian POWs, Jews and various other political and racial prisoners. The work camps made Auschwitz a huge financial enterprise. Profits were gained on everything from the personal possessions of the dead (including their clothes, jewellery, gold teeth, glasses and hair) through to forced labour for major German companies such as Krupp, Siemens-Schuckert and I.G. Farben.

A combination of crushing hard work, minimal medical attention, guard brutality and starvation meant that inmate survival was usually measured in a matter of weeks, even if he or she had avoided going to the gas chambers. These were contained in the camp's extermination centre, Auschwitz II (Birkenau). The killing and body disposal facilities (crematoriums) here regularly expanded, taking the daily death tolls from around 1,000 in 1941 up to 12,000 innocent human beings in 1943.

ABOVE: A haunting display at Auschwitz of the blue and white uniforms worn by inmates, or at least those who were not immediately killed upon arrival. The uniforms were thin and provided no protection against the cold winter months.

LEFT: The main gate at Auschwitz concentration camp. The now infamous sign across the entrance reads 'Arbeit macht frei' – 'Work makes you free'. The slogan was given directly by Rudolf Höss, the Auschwitz commandant, although the way he intended it to be interpreted by prisoners is uncertain.

LEFT: Canisters of Zyklon-B: the deadly cyanide-based gas used in the gas chambers became active on contact with air.

The peak of Auschwitz's extermination programme came in 1944. As the war turned against Germany, there was a furious effort to purge Hungary in particular of its Jewish population. Auschwitz began to receive mass Hungarian deportations, almost all for gassing, in May 1944. By July 1944, just two months later, 400,000 Hungarian Jews had been murdered.

Mass killings continued in Auschwitz until early November 1944, when they ceased under orders direct from Himmler as the Soviets advanced towards Germany from the east. Auschwitz was finally liberated on 27 January 1945. The subsequent revelations of what went on there, broadcast through the world's media, have haunted humanity ever since.

RIGHT: 26 May 1944. On the railway platform of Auschwitz-Birkenau, hundreds of Hungarian Jews are divided into two columns. They are undergoing the selection process, in which the SS guards will decide who will live and who will die.

Mass Murder

The murder of six million Jews was a huge enterprise, far beyond the means of just a few key Nazi officials. Indeed, the scale of involvement by both Germans and non-Germans is one of the most challenging aspects of this dark period in history, defying our sense of what it takes for societies and individuals to perform evil actions.

Throughout occupied Europe, local participation in the 'Final Solution' often amounted to official government policy. Antisemitism was far from confined only to Germany, and collaboration with the Nazis was motivated by factors that included racial ideology and greed to acquire Jewish goods and property. It ranged from simple acts of administration, such as compiling lists of Jewish citizens for deportation, through to active participation in killings. During the German invasion of Lithuania, for example, Germans often stood and watched as Lithuanian civilians crudely murdered local Jews in town squares, and throughout the occupied territories of the Soviet Union, SS *Einsatzgruppen* were heavily assisted by local police units, who often provided some of the most merciless killers. As the war progressed the SS itself was heavily padded out by foreign soldiers: by 1945, 26 *Waffen-SS* divisions were either partly or wholly foreign.

The SS

Led by Heinrich Himmler, the SS was the Nazi Party's paramilitary wing, originally formed as Hitler's personal bodyguard in the 1920s. It grew to a size second only to the German Army, and was divided into the more administrative *Allgemeine-SS* (General SS) and the *Waffen-SS* (Armed SS), the latter being an active combat unit. Collectively the SS played a huge part in the Holocaust, from conducting *Einsatzgruppen* operations through to running the concentration and extermination camps. SS personnel were, on the whole, utterly loyal to Adolf Hitler, and were completely indoctrinated in Nazi racial theory, hence they willingly committed many of the worst crimes against the Jewish people.

Concentration and extermination camps also came to rely upon foreign personnel, especially Ukrainians – many of whom falsely identified the Jewish people as responsible for the persecutions and famines they had experienced under Stalin.

Collaboration extended to local and national governments on occasions. Slovakia, Croatia and Romania (Germany's allies) all aided the Nazi deportation and extermination programmes with

LEFT: The Nazis continued their programme of deportation and extermination well into 1944. Here we see the deportation of Jews from Budapest, Hungary. From 1941 all Jews were steadily forced to identify themselves with a yellow cloth star bearing the word 'Jude', as seen on the man in the centre.

ABOVE: A cattle wagon typical of those used to transport people to the concentration camps. Prisoners would be packed in so tightly that there was often only standing room. After an average journey lasting 4–5 days, but with ordeals of up to 18 days being recorded, many of a train's occupants would be dead on arrival.

RIGHT: Children destined for deportation to the concentration camps look out fearfully from the side of a goods wagon. Up to 1.5 million children under the age of 16 were murdered by the Nazis during the Holocaust.

scant encouragement. (Romanian death squads, for example, killed 100,000 Jews from Bukovina and Bessarabia.) Vichy France was more than helpful in expelling Jews, including thousands who had fled from pre-war Germany – some 90,000 French and foreign Jews were therefore sent to their doom in the camps.

For the Nazis, the greatest logistical challenges of the 'Final Solution' were detaining, confining, then deporting their victims. Numerous party and civilian organizations were involved in this process, including the Gestapo, SS, civil servants, railway officials, record-keeping departments and,

at times, the regular German armed forces. The security services and police would also track down Jews in hiding, relying principally on informants to unearth their victims. Planning was critical, especially in terms of timetabling arrivals at the death camps – arrivals could not significantly exceed the speed of killing without creating a security problem for the camp authorities. Yet the efforts of people such as Adolf Eichmann, the SS officer responsible for much of the Nazi deportation programme, meant that the gas chambers and crematoriums were kept busy with the killing of innocent people.

Life and Death in the Camps

eath was literally everywhere in the concentration and extermination camps. Starving inmates were held in barracks consisting of nothing more than wooden bunks, in which diseases such as typhus proliferated. The living literally slept alongside the dead, the latter being dragged out in the morning and stacked up in courtyards ready for burning. Guard brutality was incessant. Individuals were shot for the slightest offence, or even on a whim. Starvation and exhaustion claimed hundreds of lives every day.

Life for the prisoners was inhumane. In the extermination camps, for example, the Germans created *Sonderkommando* (Special Units), groups of Jewish inmates selected for the heartbreaking and horrifying task of body disposal. This involved entering a gas chamber packed with up to 1,000 dead people, dragging them outside and transporting them away for burial or cremation. The *Sonderkommando* members were themselves constantly replaced, each man eventually shot or gassed and burned just like those he had handled – the Nazis didn't want any witnesses. In several camps the Nazis also used Jewish people for horrible medical experiments that usually resulted in the deaths of those enduring them.

Staying alive in such camps was largely a matter of luck – being posted to the right labour section, having a skill useful to the Germans, managing to obtain a little more food. Yet incredibly, even in such appalling circumstances, the Jews managed to cling to certain aspects of their humanity and culture. Secretly, many Jews conducted religious rites and even marriage ceremonies in places as apparently godless as Auschwitz, indicating something of the remarkable human instinct for spiritual survival. In five of the extermination camps, the Nazi guards formed orchestras from talented Jewish musicians, forcing them to play while their fellow Jews went to the gas chambers. Although the use of their talent was tragic, they undoubtedly

Humanity in the camps

Eugene Heimler, a survivor of several Nazi camps, remembered that in Buchenwald he met some inmates who had opted for arrest rather than turn on Jews:

Then I was taken to this Block 23. Next to us, but approachable, were the Danish police in their military Danish uniform. They were deported because they were unwilling to deport the Jews to the Gestapo, so 'en bloc' they are giving themselves up, march into the Gestapo headquarters, and from there they were taken to Buchenwald. Proud, decent people. One policeman by the name of Nils Almach was very friendly with me. By that time the winter was coming and he gave me ... one of the spare military uniforms, underwear, trousers, what you have, and military cap. And also he gave me from his rations, part of his rations. So that helped.

LEFT: Emaciated prisoners in the Buchenwald concentration camp lie next to one another in their wooden bunks. The barracks in which they lived were unheated, and diseases such as typhus and cholera proliferated in such insanitary conditions.

RIGHT: Three members of the *Sonderkommando* – Jews forced to work in the extermination process – stand by the side of a machine used to crush up the bones of the dead.

BELOW: Home-made playing cards, and 'love buttons' – a device used to pass messages between prisoners in concentration camps.

brought some beauty to the ears of those about to die. Minor acts of defiance were constant. Jews literally walking to their deaths would tear up their money, to prevent the Nazis benefiting from it. A letter written by an executed *Sonderkommando* member, Chaim Hermann, to his wife and daughter, explained that even though he knew his death was certain, he was leaving 'calmly and perhaps heroically'. Another *Sonderkommando* member risked his life to give his cousin, who was literally about to be executed, a can of meat so that he didn't go to his death hungry. Survivor testimony speaks of hundreds of such acts of kindness and defiance, and there are doubtless thousands more that have gone untold.

RIGHT: A pile of shoes – some of the 80,000 pairs that are held in Auschwitz to this day – serve as a stark reminder of the human cost of the Holocaust. The Nazis recycled shoe leather for various civilian and military applications.

The Ghettos and Jewish Resistance

The confinement of Jews in urban ghettos was a key element of Nazi racial policy from 1939. At first, ghettos were more about containment rather than preparation for extermination, but by the end of 1941 they became a transit stage to the extermination camps and labour camps.

Ghettos were established in many occupied territories, for example Theresienstadt in Czechoslovakia, but the largest, Warsaw and Lodz, were in what had been Poland. The ghettos were in essence sealed portions of a town or city, often based around existing Jewish quarters, in which Jews were isolated. Although the ghettos were under overall German control, the Nazis ordered the appointment of *Judenrate* (Jewish Councils) responsible for ensuring that Nazi directives were followed. Conditions were generally appalling. In Warsaw, overcrowding led to about 15 people occupying every room. Poor sanitation generated widespread disease which – combined with a lack of food (at times less than 300 calories a day) – meant that more than 43,000 people died in the Warsaw ghetto alone in 1941.

Generally speaking, Jewish resistance to ghettoization and deportation was localized rather than widespread. Yet there were key moments of vigorous resistance. An uprising in Warsaw between 19 April and 15 May 1943 inflicted serious casualties on the Germans before it was finally quashed and the ghetto destroyed. Later in the war, there were even short-lived but vigorous uprisings in the Treblinka and Sobibor

extermination camps and the Bialystok ghetto. These were brutally suppressed, but they remind us that not all Jews went to their fate with forced compliance. The Sobibor uprising, for example, on 14 October 1943, saw 600 slave labourers attempt a breakout. While only 84 of them survived the escape and the remaining war, they became symbols of resistance. More broadly, individual Jews, or humane non-Jews, performed numerous acts of defiance against the Nazis throughout the occupied territories and amongst

ABOVE: A small Jewish boy busks with his violin in the Warsaw ghetto in 1941, hoping to be given some food or money.

LEFT: Housing conditions in many of the ghettos became horribly cramped. Here, in the ghetto of Kutno in Poland, one family has converted a rusted car into a makeshift home.

RIGHT: SS units round up Jewish families during the final Nazi liquidation of the Jewish ghetto in Warsaw in April 1943. SS General Jürgen Stroop, who was in charge of the operation, afterwards wrote in his report, 'There is no Jewish residential district in Warsaw anymore.'

BELOW: During the Warsaw ghetto uprising of 1943, a group of SS troops stand guard over Jews found sheltering in a basement. Stroop claimed 17 German soldiers were killed and around 100 injured during the uprising (although Jewish and Polish sources put the figures much higher), while tens of thousands of Warsaw's Jews were either killed in the city or deported to the extermination camps.

The Bielski Resistance

In December 1941, four Jewish brothers – Tuvia, Asael, Aron and Zus Bielski – fled from the Nowogrodek ghetto in Western Belorussia after their parents and two other brothers were murdered by the Nazis. They formed a partisan group in the Zabielovo and Perelaz forests. At first they focused mainly on protecting family and friends, but eventually they came to be responsible for sheltering, at the group's peak, 1,230 Jewish people who had escaped from German clutches. The Bielski camp was highly organized, and included a school, hospital, kitchen, flour mill and bakery, although it was constantly on the move as the Germans conducted huge anti-partisan operations. A combat unit within the group also destroyed bridges, attacked German convoys, disabled German trains and killed local collaborators. Asael later died fighting for the Soviet Army in February 1945, while the remaining three brothers, after the war, emigrated to Israel and then the United States.

the Allied armed forces. In the East, gangs of fugitive Jews formed partisan or survivor groups in the wilderness, some of significant size (see panel). In France, 3,000 Jews were given sanctuary in the village of Le Chambon-sur-Lignon and eventually escaped across the border into Switzerland. Thousands of Jewish soldiers from Palestine also served in the British Army, fighting in North Africa and Italy against German forces. (A Jewish Brigade Group was established in September 1944.) In the Soviet forces, the 16th Lithuanian Division was entirely manned by Jewish personnel. Such resistance from thousands of Jews ensured that the Nazi domination of the Jewish people was never total.

Outside Knowledge

The extent to which the Allies and ordinary Germans knew about the Holocaust is a frequently heated debate. What cannot be doubted is that the general German population was fully aware of Jewish persecution and deportation, even if the Jews' final destination was an ominous mystery. Many ordinary Germans were at some point directly involved in the processes that led to the concentration camps, be they dutiful railway clerks or businessmen involved in exploiting camp labour. More explicitly, the thousands of men (and some women) involved directly in extermination operations, or the hundreds of thousands of regular German soldiers who witnessed such operations in the occupied territories, did occasionally write home to loved ones about what was going on, or send photographs. Polish postal workers in 1942, for instance, found a German soldier's letter home with an accompanying photograph of an *Einsatzgruppe* unit in action, showing a German policeman about to shoot a woman holding her infant child, while other Ukrainian peasants dig their own graves. Everything combined, by 1943 the German population would at least have a general awareness that the Jews' trip to the east was terminal.

Looking further afield, how much did the Allies know about what was happening? In 1941–42, reports from Polish, Soviet and Swiss sources, and from code-breaking successes, provided the first clear evidence of systematic exterminations. At first such reports were treated with incredulity or were ignored. Yet even when the weight of evidence later became overwhelming, the Allied reaction to genocide was largely muted and ineffective. In 1944, for example, when it became evident that Hungary was being purged of its Jews, the British initially refused refuge for Jews in Palestine. American pressure eventually forced the British to issue 5,000 immigration certificates.

A further ineffective response came from the Vatican. Pope Pius XII never issued any overt statement condemning the persecution. A combination of religious prejudice, a general affection for Germany (he had served there as a papal ambassador) and a fear of communism (to which the Nazis were implacably opposed) probably

ABOVE: Foreign awareness of what was happening to the Jews was aided by the thousands of foreign volunteers who served in Himmler's SS, as frontline combat troops, *Einsatzgruppen* members and as concentration camp guards. The men here are Bosnian soldiers of the 13th *Waffen-SS* Mountain Division 'Handschar'.

ABOVE: Luggage is piled high as Hungarian Jews continue to arrive in Auschwitz, 26 May 1944.

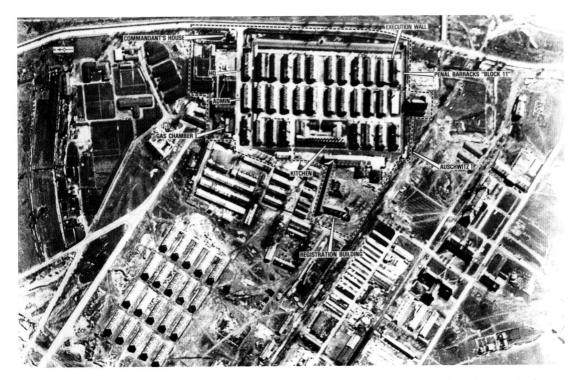

ABOVE: An Allied aerial photograph of the Auschwitz concentration camp, taken on 4 April 1944. It clearly shows the many prisoner barracks and also indicates the location of a gas chamber.

Oskar Schindler (1908–74)

Austro-German industrialist Oskar Schindler has been remembered as the saviour of some 1,300 Jews. A hard-drinking, womanizing gambler, who socialized with the local Nazi elite, he initially made serious money in occupied Poland by using Jewish labour in his Deutsche Emaillewaren-Fabrik (DEF) factory in Krakow. Witnessing Nazi brutality, however, changed Schindler, and his factories became a refuge for Jewish workers, where they were free from violence and inhuman working conditions, and were properly fed. As the war progressed, and particularly after the liquidation of the Krakow ghetto, Schindler had to work hard to prevent his workers being deported to death camps, and even secured the transfer of Jews out of Plaszow concentration camp, commanded by the brutal SS officer Amon Göth. Schindler's efforts bankrupted him, and he would die penniless in 1974. Today, however, he has been given the Israeli honour of 'Righteous among the Nations'.

ABOVE: The famous Oskar Schindler saved about 1,300 Jews by sheltering them within his factory system in Poland. Here he sits, in 1974, with one of the people he saved (left) when she had been just a child.

account for his inaction, but it was of lasting damage to his reputation.

In defence of the weak responses of the Allies, we have to acknowledge that the Holocaust took place within a wider war that would eventually kill an estimated 56 million people. During this life-and-death struggle the focus of effort was on winning the war and crushing the Nazi regime and, as appalling as it was, saving Jews was not the Allies' immediate priority.

Nearing the End: 1943–1945

By the end of 1943, the war had turned irrevocably against Nazi Germany. In retreat on all fronts, the Nazis realized that their crimes would potentially soon be exposed. By this time, *Einsatzgruppen* and police units on the Eastern Front had already made some efforts to hide previous activities. SS officer Paul Blobel was commissioned as early as June 1942 to remove all traces of killings in the east. He used unfortunate Russian POWs to exhume thousands of corpses and burn them in vast pits. The scale of the murders, however, meant that the attempts to eradicate all their tracks were less than successful, and the woodlands, ravines and fields of the Soviet Union would provide plenty more evidence for war crimes trials after the war. The remains of 1,000 children, for example, lie unexhumed in a mass grave in Vinnitsa, Ukraine, to this day.

In late 1943, the concentration camp commanders also accepted that it was time to conceal evidence – the Sobibor camp, for one, was dismantled and the ground planted with trees. Treblinka and Belzec camps were also destroyed

in 1943. At Auschwitz, the last execution selection was performed in October 1944 before, on 2 November, Himmler ordered all killings of Jews to stop. The Auschwitz gas chambers were blown up shortly thereafter.

That order came too late for almost all of the Jewish population of German-occupied Europe – most camp survivors by the beginning of 1945 were not Jews but Soviet POWs and forced labourers of many other nationalities. Substantial evacuations of inmates from Auschwitz and other camps had already begun by this time. Many of those prisoners who were evacuated from the camps subsequently endured the further horrors of forced marches, travelling for days on end with little food and water, and executed immediately

BELOW: Gassings at Auschwitz continued well into the autumn of 1944, despite the fact that by this time the war had turned decisively against Germany. Here we see the arrival of Hungarian Jews on 26 May 1944. *Sonderkommando* inmates, in striped uniforms, were forced to help take away the arrivals' possessions.

LEFT: A gas chamber at Auschwitz-Birkenau, blown up by the guards in January 1945 in a futile attempt to hide the camp's crimes.

BELOW: All is quiet; the deserted concentration camp at Auschwitz-Birkenau. The camp was liberated by Soviet forces on 27 January 1945, who found 7,000 remaining prisoners, typically those who had been too weak to embark on the death march west.

if they lagged behind or fell exhausted. Of the *c.* 700,000 prisoners evacuated from camps in January 1945, it is believed that about 250,000 died during the death marches west. Those who did make it to Germany were usually forced temporarily into camps of near-equal depravity, such as Buchenwald, Sachsenhausen and Dachau, where thousands more perished, or began further death marches.

Yet although the killing of Jews and other camp inmates continued in various forms unabated, there was little doubt that the Allied armies were closing around Nazi Germany. Soon the full extent of what had been perpetrated would be revealed.

Death march

Concentration camp inmate Olga Albogen tells of a death march from Neustadt to Bergen-Belsen in 1945, during which a train journey brought no respite:

So finally they got us into a train, but in Hannover it was bombed by the Allies and a lot of people died there, and it took a few days until we could move on from there. Without food, without anything. And then they got us open wagons, you know, cattle cars, whatever they were, but open-topped. Just half. So it was crowded and going for days, it seemed like forever. The snow was falling on us. We had hardly any clothes on. Daytime the sun came out and the snow was melting on us, into our clothes, body. And as evening came, the night came, it was freezing again and froze on us.

ABOVE: A German memorial remembers those who died on the death march from Dachau in April 1945. Approximately 7,000 prisoners began the long trek, but hundreds died during the journey, despite passing through numerous German villages where shelter and food was just metres away.

Liberation and Justice

The first concentration camp liberated by the Allies was Majdanek, which was captured virtually intact by Soviet forces in July 1944, despite some German efforts to destroy it before leaving. The last was Stutthof, located near Danzig, which did not pass into Allied hands until 9 May 1945. Between these two events was a steady revelation of extermination and cruelty that stunned even a war-weary world.

The sights that greeted the Allied soldiers defied belief. Indeed, some media authorities back in Britain and the United States initially resisted broadcasting the revelations, fearing that the reports were communist-inspired exaggerations. Yet once the British and US soldiers saw the reality for themselves, there could be no doubt.

At Majdanek, where some 200,000 people had died, the Soviet liberation exposed gas chambers (their walls stained blue by Zyklon-B gas, cans of which were found unopened), crematoria for disposing of bodies, a pile of hundreds of thousands of discarded shoes, and about 1,000 emaciated prisoners. Even greater horrors awaited at other camps – huge piles of human hair, glasses and gold teeth; endless piles of corpses, such as those graphically filmed at Bergen-Belsen. Tens of thousands of people still died after liberation – of typhus, dysentery, malnutrition and years of abuse. At Bergen-Belsen, the death rate was about 300 people every day.

Along with the revelations of crimes came a desire for justice and retribution. Sometimes this was immediate. In Dachau, enraged US soldiers

ABOVE: The British troops who liberated Bergen-Belsen were faced with murder on an unimaginable scale. Here hundreds of Jews lie in a mass grave, just a fraction of the 60,000 people who died in the camp.

executed more than one hundred SS guards on the spot, until commanders intervened. In some camps, the inmates exacted their revenge, clubbing or stabbing their gaolers to death.

More formal justice took a slower course. At subsequent war crimes trials, most famously those at Nuremberg between 1945 and 1949, dozens of contributors to the Holocaust were tried. Many, from the commandant of Auschwitz to *Einsatzgruppen* leaders and Nazi doctors, were found guilty and either executed or sentenced to life imprisonment. Both Hitler and Himmler, however, escaped through suicide. For others, justice came

LEFT: Following the liberation of his camp by the US 3rd Armored Division, a concentration camp inmate points out a guard who was noted for his brutal beatings of prisoners. In several camps guards were killed by either Allied soldiers or inmates following liberation.

ABOVE: Smiles and cheers as American troops liberate survivors from the concentration camp at Dachau on 29 April 1945.

ABOVE: Senior figures from the Nazi leadership face the International Military Tribunal at Nuremberg in 1945, charged with war crimes. While hundreds of Nazis connected with the Holocaust were tried, many thousands more who participated slipped through the net and led free lives.

long after the war. Adolf Eichmann, for example, was abducted by Israeli agents in Argentina in 1960, flown covertly back to Israel, then tried and executed. Former SS officers and camp guards have been tracked down and prosecuted into the beginning of the 21st century, the passage of time in no way diminishing their crimes.

Dignity in liberation

Edith Birkin, a concentration camp survivor, here recounts her feelings about the German guards following the British liberation of Bergen-Belsen (the camp in which she was finally held):

The British got these carts with Germans inside them; they had to pick up the bodies and then sit on top of the bodies, go a little further, get off, pick up some more bodies, get on top of these bodies you know. And that's a wonderful wonderful sight, to see these Germans that I knew were so horrible and so sadistic, sitting on top of these bodies, having to pick them up. I wasn't feeling vindictive; I could have taken stones and thrown, some people did. I never threw a stone at them or anything, I didn't … didn't want to lower myself to that.

Tolls and Effects

The human cost of the Holocaust is numbing to consider. Between 1941 and 1945, the Nazi Party, aided by numerous sectors of the regular armed forces and by the civilian administration, systematically murdered around 6 million Jews. In some countries almost the entire Jewish population was wiped out. Poland, for example, had a total Jewish population of around 3.3 million at the beginning of the war. By 1945, an estimated 3 million of those people were dead. The Netherlands had a population of 150,000 Jews reduced to about 35,000 by the Nazi deportations and executions, and Hungary's Jews were reduced by 70 per cent in just a few months. We do not know fully how many Soviet Jews were killed, but the likely final death toll is at least 1.1 million, and possibly as high as 2.2 million. Nor was it only the Jewish people who suffered under the mechanisms of the 'Final Solution'. Some 224,000 Gypsies were also murdered, and about 60 per cent of Soviet POWs were worked and starved to death – around 3.5 million men. Minority groups targeted included Jehovah's Witnesses – 6,000 died in the camps – plus unknown numbers whom the Nazis termed 'undesirables', such as homeless people, homosexuals and petty criminals.

The generational effects of the Holocaust are incalculable. To look at this perspective in reverse, it is estimated that the 1,300 Jews saved by Oskar Schindler (see page 25) have produced some 7,000 descendants. The murder of nearly 70 per cent of all European Jews, therefore, has had a profound effect on the Jewish global population to this day.

For those who survived, life remained far from easy. Many returned from concentration camps to find that their homes had comfortable new occupants who were unwilling to hand their gains back. Antisemitism also persisted – in Poland, for example, 1,500 Jews were murdered in violent attacks by Polish citizens in the 12 months following the end of the war. Consequently, most Jews had to build new lives from virtually penniless beginnings. Many emigrated abroad, particularly to the United States and the new State of Israel, established in 1948. Israel once more became the Jewish homeland, although one beleaguered by ongoing war with neighbouring Arab states.

Regardless of where they went, however, thousands of concentration camp survivors carried with them appalling psychological problems for the rest of their lives, haunted

LEFT: A new life. A total of 1,204 Jewish survivors of the Holocaust arrive aboard a British ship at the port of Haifa in 1945, in what was at the time the British Mandate for Palestine. The State of Israel was subsequently born in 1948, and many of those who had emigrated from Europe found themselves fighting in a war against hostile Arab nations.

by the enormity of the evil they witnessed. Their pain passed to subsequent generations – offspring of Holocaust survivors were found to have increased risk of clinical depression, bred from witnessing their parents' nightmares and hearing their stories. Yet the fact remains that the survivors built a new life for themselves, displaying the courage, resilience and dignity to start again. Given history, however, the Jewish people are likely to remain forever guarded.

ABOVE: One of the millions. Helene Berr, a Jewish student and writer from France, wrote about her experiences in a powerful diary. She was eventually deported to Auschwitz then to Bergen-Belsen, where she died just days before its liberation.

Estimated death tolls of Jews, 1941–45

Country	Pre-war Jewish population	Jews murdered by the Nazis
Albania	2,000	600
Austria	191,000	65,000
Belgium	100,000	28,500
Baltic States	255,000	228,000
Bulgaria	50,000	14,000
Czechoslovakia	360,000	180,000
Denmark	8,000	120
France	300,000	90,000
Germany	240,000	200,000
Greece	75,000	60,000
Holland	150,000	102,000
Hungary	650,000	450,000
Italy	75,000	15,000
Luxembourg	5,000	1,000
Norway	2,200	1,000
Poland	3.3 million	3 million
Romania	600,000	300,000
USSR	4.7 million	At least 1.1 million
Yugoslavia	75,000	55,000

RIGHT: A US soldier inspects the tragic loot of the Holocaust – thousands of gold wedding rings taken from the victims of the extermination camps. Each ring represents a couple torn apart, and often children separated from their parents.

Remembering

The enormity of the Holocaust has meant that it is today one of the most studied events in history. Yet for all the many books, films, articles and documentaries produced, it seems that the fundamental explanation for how thousands of people could participate in industrial-scale slaughter still eludes us. At its heart, the Holocaust is as much about how people behave as it is about the politics and ideologies of the time.

Rightly, the history and testimony of the Holocaust are perpetuated by major museums and institutions, such as Yad Vashem in Israel and the US Holocaust Memorial Museum (USHMM) in Washington DC. Several former extermination and concentration camps, including Auschwitz and Dachau, are kept as living, haunting museums of the past, receiving and influencing hundreds of thousands of visitors every year. The United Kingdom holds a Holocaust Memorial Day on 27 January every year.

Such remembrances are essential. Since 1945, a dark thread of Holocaust denial has emerged, typically amongst far right 'historians' looking to rehabilitate the Nazi ideology and discredit the Jewish people. Holocaust denial has no historical basis, but has to be combated nevertheless.

The last word here goes to Anne Frank, the Jewish girl who hid from the Nazis for two years in Amsterdam before being arrested and deported to Auschwitz and the Bergen-Belsen camp, where she died, aged 15, of typhus. In her now-famous diary, written in Amsterdam before her arrest, she declared, 'Despite everything, I believe that people are really good at heart.' Such hope is fragile, but worth holding on to.

ABOVE: A school party visits Auschwitz concentration camp in 2009. Educating successive generations about the Holocaust is vital to help guard against potential genocides of the future.

RIGHT: At this monument at Treblinka, some of the 17,000 stones are carved with the names of Polish villages and communities devastated by the Holocaust. The upright structure in the background, representing a tombstone, is on the site of the gas chamber that once stood here. The death camp was dismantled by the Nazis in 1943.